GET FINISHED:

Volume One

By: Deona Benson

Hebrews 12:1 "And let us run with patience the race that

is set before us."

Unless otherwise noted, scripture quotations are from The King James Version of Scripture.

Published in Oxford, MS by Due Date Ministries

Cover by Roderickus Pickens

Printed in the United States of America

Dedication

This book is dedicated to my father, my dad, my daddy, my mentor. One of the greatest men on earth; a super hero in my eyes, Apostle Darnell Thompson. Whenever I need a person of flesh to prove that endurance is possible, I look to you. In times that I become weary, frustrated, and discouraged with not only life but in well doing, you are the walking scripture that reminds me to be not weary for there is a due season. Your fight for life, your pursuit for purpose, your relentless faithfulness and your unwavering determination to GET FINISHED will always be my inspiration. Thank you for your example. Thank you for allowing your love and faith in God to be your guiding light. Since I was a little girl you showed me a man of faith, is a faithful man. Your reward is great I have no doubt! You have certainly run and continue to run as one to obtain a prize! Your seeds reach far and wide.

Mike Murdock in his book of *101 Wisdom Keys* said, "The seed that leaves your hand will never leave your life." I believe it! Thank you for the countless seeds you have sown. Thank you for not only preaching the Gospel, but for living the gospel. I anticipate the explosion of God's blessings in your life! For the past 17 years, I have watched you Pastor with passion. I have listened to your profound revelation of the Grace of God. It is from that truth and your example that I am determined to GET FINISHED!

Thank you for helping me to realize that we are Living Inside of Grace, your life is the book that you aspire to write!

To you I give a round of applause and a standing ovation!

Acknowledgements

I start by first acknowledging my heavenly father, the King and creator of all things. I thank you for trusting me with this assignment. I thank you for the divine inspiration and ability through the Holy Spirit to bring this first volume to completion. My life is no longer my own and forever I will lend my heart and my pen to you.

To my amazing husband, the man that I get to spend the rest of my life with. Together we've faced the challenge to get Finished. Together we've cried and individually we've concealed our tears to be strength for each other. We have seen some low times, physically, mentally and emotionally. Our faith was developed through the fire. We were developed through the fire. Thanks be to God who saw us through, gave us hope, extended his grace, and encouraged us to run on to see the end. We have done great things together, but I want to take this time to encourage you. You see, I've watched you battle, fight, hurt, and yet endure. I saw you face death and walk with your head up. I saw you cry without releasing tears to encourage me. With my own eyes, I witnessed you seek God to lead us. You are a purpose pusher, you are anointed to cause others to get up and walk. Your passion and persistence in doing what God has called you to do his way is one of the things I admire most about you. I call you my David, as you are indeed worshipper and king. Your humility is impeccable. I appreciate how you choose God in a generation that competition and vain glory is trying to infiltrate the church and the minds of those that carry God's assignments. Thank you for making God enough in your life and seeking his heart without wavering. Thank you for staying in the race! Thank you for the hope you give our family, our church and to everyone that is privileged to be impacted by your voice! It is my pleasure that God has chosen me to be your wife! I love you with a love that cannot be put in to words! The world will see, hear, know and be impacted by you! Thank you for allowing the impact to be first felt in our home. You survived for a generation!

Get Finished!

To my children, Nathan, Aubrey, Noah, and Madison. It is with a love that I can't express that I love you. It is a real love; a love that has no limits. It is a love that vows to be ever present and ever faithful. It is a love that will cover and protect. I vow to be the voice that will always speak to the Kings and Queens in you. I vow to be the voice you can count on. You are not only my children but my ministry, and I'm honored that God chose me for you! As you grow, you will understand the depth of the words in this book. Let me sum it up like this: you are here on purpose. To find that purpose, you must find God and accept Jesus as your savior. When you find your purpose, let nothing stop you!! BE GREAT! GREATNESS is who you are! Dream Big! Life is beautiful so LIVE! God is always with you and so am I.

To my mother Yma Thompson, my beautiful mother, thank you! Thank you for being the one who holds dad up! You are the link to every great thing in my life. Your presence, prayers, words, counsel, love, wisdom, support, and some part of you have influenced everything that has influenced me. I am not sure if you know how valuable you are to the equation, but you are! Without you, I probably wouldn't have the things I appreciate most. It is your position that kept me in mine. Thank you for following so well, that you had impact on the lead! There is no other woman like you and you could never be replaced! Your beauty runs much deeper than what can be seen. Thank you for pressing, get ready for Bethel, God has indeed provided a resting place!

To my family, by blood and by love, siblings, Beyond the Break Mentorship members, my amazing church family and friends: there would be more pages in the acknowledgements than in the book if I named you by name. I appreciate your love, your push, and your prayers. Special thanks to my spiritual children Kordarius and Toi for the many ways and days that you encouraged me to GET FINISHED with this assignment! Your seeds will come back to you in a much greater measure than you can imagine! My mother and father in love Emma and Ellis, also my late grandmother Velma Wilson. Grandma I couldn't dare write a book and not mention the voice that would have cheered the loudest! I miss you so much! This one's for you!

To two special friends in my life, Prophetess Cycelia Matthews and Pastor Sherri Livingston, from the moment of our friendship we've been sisters. The two of you have not only extended your love and loyalty but you have unselfishly extended doors to me. It is because of you that I have many of the connections and doors opened that I do. You both have consistently ministered to me and helped me to deliver. Your prayers and support helped to guide me through this assignment. I will never forget how you've helped me. Thank you for being favor in my life.

Lastly, my Bishop, Bishop Roderick Mitchell and Pastor Mary Mitchell, it is your wisdom that I used as a guide throughout the pages of this book. I am wise enough to know the benefits of a covering, thank you for being positioned that I might receive those benefits! Thank you

for your presence that has been such a present in my life!

Table of Contents

Introduction

Perhaps it's planting a garden, remodeling a kitchen, or building a shed. Maybe it's finishing school, a project, or a business venture. We can all relate to the beginning of a thing. For some, getting started is the greatest giant. You know what you need or would like to do, but something has you stuck. You have instructions, but you're still in park. Then there are those that make it seem as if starting is easy breezy. You have a list of projects, businesses, or groups you've organized. Many books you've started to write, and things around the home you've taken apart with a plan to complete a certain task. In the history of starts there are also a list of stops; not because the work was completed, but because starting and stopping is a cycle for you. There are also those of you who are called to tasks that you struggle with how to begin. Here is one that's probably the most common, and that is those that are gripped with fear. Fear has brought about complacency and you simply can't see yourself doing much of anything unless you can do it in the absence of the participation, or witness from others. Perhaps it's the fear of failure that has held you up and caused you to be fruitless. The fact is that, this world is a great big world full of people that are filled with potential that don't know how to move beyond circumstance. Many people across the world live life half way. They never crack the surface of possibilities in order to see the abundance that is not only accessible to them, but also waiting to come through them; moving them from existence to abundantly living a life fulfilled and purposed.

Failure, insecurity, shame, condemnation, lack, poverty, fear, confusion, chaos, pride, intimidation, excuses, lies from the enemy, are all just a few reasons why the earth's population out number the seeds of purpose that we, those that God has released in the earth, have sown into her ground. Far too many people are dying pregnant with purpose, and far too many people are alive, and yet barren. Your life is more than a social security number and economic status. Your life is the very purpose of Christ. Our release in the earth was appointed intentionally. You were called to impact territory and to change culture. The very year, month, and day that you were born is significant. God needed a you in the earth for such a time as this. God didn't just breathe life into you, he breathed purpose for living. His breath released the same "let there be" authority as was in the beginning. You are a "let there be." Inside of you is a "let there be." There is something depending on you in order to be released. Something great is anticipating to breakout through you. What "let there be" are you carrying? For Danny Thomas, it was St. Jude's Research Center. For Sam Walton, it was Walmart. For George Williams, it was YMCA. For me, it was this book. My "let there be" is to pull out the "let there be" inside of you.

What "let there be" is inside of you? There's not just one, but there are multiple! Multiple seeds of potential, multiple gifts, and multiple miracles are inside of you. They are trying to break out. They need your push and your persistence. They need breath, your breath. The process has begun because you're breathing, but the process is not complete until your "let there be" is breathing too.

Whether you have acknowledged it or not, your life is for God's use and his glory. If you are a believer in Christ, Romans 8:9 tells us that our lives are no longer our own. We've been bought with a price; here to impact the earth and expand the kingdom. This book is purposed to awaken purpose, purpose in you. This book is also written to help guide you as you lay hold of what has been laid before you. It's not only to get you started, but also to focus you on the finish. It's time for you to run, be fruitful, increase, and subdue, so that every good work will be brought to completion.

Let us Pray

Heavenly Father,

Together we are entering a journey. A journey that will
cause us to function as you in the earth. We know that
according to your word, we are created in your image and
in your likeness. We want to represent you in all that we
do. We want to bring glory to your name and your glorious
image. Lord, you are the finisher, you completed every
good work that was set before you. Not only did you
complete the work set before you, but the word of God
also tells us that you will complete the work that you have
begun in us. As we read the pages of this book, we prepare
our hearts to be active participants of your work with
endurance, patience, diligence, and faith to finish what you
have called us to do. We thank you that these words and

instructions will not only be read and received, but we thank you that we will read, receive, and conceive. We will bring forth fruit and fruit that will remain. We thank you for fanning the flame on the inside of us. We yield to you now. Speak to the place in us that you have ordained to come forth for your glory.

In Jesus' Name,

Amen

Chapter One

Get the Instructions

Judges 13:7-8 NLT

But he told me, You will become pregnant and give birth to a son, You must not drink wine or any other alcoholic drink nor eat any forbidden food. For your son will be dedicated to God as a Nazirite from the moment of his birth until the day of his death.

8) Then the Manoah prayed to the Lord saying, "Lord, please let the man of God come back to us again and give us more instructions about this son who is to be born.

In this passage of scripture, we read the prophecy concerning the birth of Samson. Manoah's wife had no children, and in an earlier verse in the chapter, it tells us that she was unable to become pregnant. One day she has a divine visitation by an angel of the Lord prophesying that she will conceive and give birth to a son. The angel is very careful and detailed about the instructions she is to follow during her pregnancy. We read that the woman's husband prayed to God that He would send back the angel with further details and instructions about the baby that would be born.

They could have very well allowed excitement to overtake them. After all, they had no children and were under Philistine oppression, so they could probably use the good news.

Though excited, Manoah said to God, I heard what you said we are to do, but we don't want to mess this up, so

2

give us the instructions concerning what we have been given.

Like Manoah and his wife, you are pregnant with purpose. You have been divinely trusted with a baby that has a "let there be" tied to it. Like Manoah, it is important that with every assignment you receive, you seek God for instructions.

Too often, we feel that God is not interested in directing us in every area of our lives, but the scripture plainly instructs us to acknowledge Him in all of our ways and He will direct our path (Proverbs 3:5-6). The Holy Spirit is so into you that He will give insight and instructions concerning something as small as putting a book shelf together, to something as large as starting a school of ministry. He is our helper, ready to guide and instruct us in all things.

I'll be honest, I had to mature in that area. I didn't always get the instructions. I was guilty of running off excitement. If you are like me, then you excite easily with the *what.* Excitement can't carry you. Only God's divine instructions are anointed and equipped to see you to the finish line.

I love God and His people, and it's my desire to see others live a fulfilled life in Christ. I love to help meet the needs of others. I am so passionate about people and seeing others encounter Christ, that I'm always thinking on ways to make this happen. My dreams are big and my imagination is bigger. Through experience, I have become strong in my faith, so it's not a challenge for me to trust God. No budget is too great, and no resources seem impossible. It causes me to be fearless. Without the wisdom of God to wait on his instructions, my fearless pursuits, though good ideas, will not be fruitful.

Without instructions, you move to lose

How much money has been lost because we moved without instructions? How much time has been wasted? How much decrease and decline have we experienced all because we were zealous, unwise, and were not patient enough to seek and receive divine instructions from God?

Instructions are marching orders. Where there are no marching orders from God, there is no leading of the Holy Spirit. Where there is no leading of the Holy Spirit, you pursue without divine purpose. Without instructions to pursue, there will be no recover. Getting the instructions is essential.

Perhaps there were things that I did not finish, because I had no grace to start because I did not have instructions. Always remember, the instructions are the what, where, and when of God. He does not always share the how. When we receive God's instructions, we must receive them with faith. Faith that says, He who spoke it will bring it to pass.

In Luke 1, when the angel appeared to Mary bringing her the divine message that she would carry the savior of the world, had she wrestled too long with the *how,* she would not have been able to fully receive the *what.* When God gives His instruction, just like Mary, our reply should be, "According to thy word be it unto me."

Agree with God's Instructions

God doesn't need your physical ability or your resources. God needs your faith. Faith's reply to God's instructions is "Yes." His only need is for us to agree with His instruction. It is when we agree by faith with God's instructions that we can begin to blaze the trail for miracles. When God gives His instructions, He needs for us to make room in our womb. Agreeing with God beyond logic, feeling, and circumstance is how we make room. Although Mary received her *how* from God, her *how* did not make sense. Her yes did not come from what made sense, it came from faith.

Agree by Faith

Just as the instructions are essential, know this, with every word from God, and every creative idea that he gives, with all divine inspiration, there must be faith application. God's instructions, though imperative for vision, don't always make sense. Therefore, it is important to know that before you have faith for things, you must have faith in God.

Perhaps you have faith for the loan to go through, but in order to not be shaken by the process, your faith must be rooted in Jehovah Jireh: the provider. Perhaps you have faith for healing, to stand on the word of God when the doctor's report gets worse before it gets better, your faith must be in Jehovah Rapha: The God that heals.

Let's consider Abraham in Genesis 22. For Abraham to obey the command of the Lord to offer his promised son up as a sacrifice, his faith had to be in God. Scripture records that after receiving the instruction of the Lord, Abraham took Isaac to the appointed place where he would carry out God's instruction. While they journeyed to that place, Isaac who did not know the details of the Lord's instructions inquired about the sacrifice. We read that Abraham responded that God would provide the sacrifice. The instruction was for Abraham to offer his son up as a sacrifice. It was because of Abraham's faith in God, he not only obeyed the instruction, but he was also able to rest in God's provision. It wasn't until Abraham was about to draw back his knife, and slay his son that God did indeed provide a sacrifice. Abraham's faith was in God alone, so he didn't get distracted by God's way. When your faith is in God, whatever you are trusting Him for will be added to you.

When you receive the instruction from God, with no question, do it God's way. Be still and hear God's voice. Search for Him. Lay hold of His plan. His way is wondrous. There is no error in Him. Following His way will keep error from you. We don't want God to bless what we are doing. We want to do what God is blessing. To every work we are called, for every purpose on the inside of us, it is all the work of the Lord. It's for His glory, it's for His purpose.

Keep God in the lead

Don't allow pride to convince you that you can do God's work without His instructions. He knows the plans He has for you. Trust His plan in such a way, that you refuse to move without it.

His plan is not just for what we view as God's business, ministry assignments, church work, etc. He has a plan for every step you will take, and for everything your hands will touch. His plan is for your life. It concerns everything that concerns you.

 Finishers are disciplined listeners. Finishers don't run with the confidence of their own sight and ability. Finishers remain confident in the ability of the Lord. Finishers seek instructions knowing that the instructions are the foundation of anything that will stand.

God's presence is in the instructions

Psalms 32:8 (AMP)

I will instruct you says the Lord and guide you along the best pathway for your life. I will advise you and watch your progress.

What a wonderful feeling it is to know that God does not only give us His instructions, but He also says, He will guide us. God's presence is in His instructions, and His instructions are for the best pathway for our lives. As He gives His instructions, His spirit goes with us, leading and advising us along the way.

Psalms 91:11 (ASV)

He will give His angels charge over you to keep you in all of your ways.

11

Don't be afraid of God's instructions. He has commanded angels to not only assist you, but they surround you, they have charge over you.

Psalms 32:8 concludes that He will keep watch over us. Sometimes the details of the instructions can be intimidating, but it is God's desire that we rest in His leading. God is watching over you, you are never alone in the details. He instructs us and He walks with us. He is always there. When it seems like He is silent, you've got to know that He is with you.

In Psalms 23 (KJV) David wrote, *Yay, though I walk through the valley of the shadow of death, I will fear no evil, FOR THOU ART WITH ME, Thy rod and thy staff, they comfort me.* The rod and the staff here can both be viewed as God's defense for us while we are in the valley against the enemy that tries to come in against us, as well as a tool to keep us in line and on the right path. So just what if God's instructions lead us to a place of what seems unfamiliar? What if following God's instructions, we find ourselves in a deep valley? David said, I fear not, because regardless of where walking with you leads me, I know that you are with me. God won't leave you alone. Before God sends you, He sends His angels before you. Psalms 91 says He gives His angels charge over you, His angels shall keep you in all of your ways.

 Before David mentioned the valley in Psalms 23, he declared that the Lord was his Shepherd.

Verse 2. *He maketh me to lie down in green pastures; He leadeth me beside the still waters.* Verse 3. *He restoreth my soul. He leadeth me in the paths of righteousness for His name sake.*

David affirmed God as a protector. His affirmation of who God is supported his faith, knowing that God would take care of him in all situations. If we acknowledge God as Shepherd, we must submit to Him as sheep.

David said that it was for God's name sake that He leads him in the paths of righteousness. God's instructions for your life has His name sake tied to them. You are destined for victory. Don't allow what you can't understand to hinder you from yielding to God's way. Proverbs 3:6 instructs us to acknowledge Him in all of our ways, and He will direct our path. A pit fall for many of us is not heeding to the instruction in Proverbs 3:7 (AMP), it says, *Be not wise in your own eyes.*

The failure to follow the instructions of God is the danger of being wise in our own eyes. The absence of humility is the presence of failure. Until we are able to count our greatest achievements and greatest abilities as nothing against the instruction of God, we will self-destruct our own pathway. Keep your ear to the heart of God.

What great glory we would experience, if we would become so dependent on the instruction of God, that we would include Him in every detail of our lives.

The plan for victory was written before you ever took one breath. Before you entered the race, He set you up for victory. God is so strategic. No failure resides in Him. He is perfect in all His ways. Be faithful to receive and obey His instructions. According to Deuteronomy 28, obedience to God's instructions will cause the blessing to overtake us. God wants to overtake you with blessings! He wants to bless you larger than you have space for. He's not just a sustaining God. He is an abundant God. His blessing brings overflow. His blessing is not just for seasonal, occasional fruit, but it is for fruit that will remain. It is to God's glory, but also our benefit that we are faithful to receive and obey His instructions. God's sheep know His voice and follow His voice. (John 10:27-29) We must keep Him in the lead!

If it can form, it can be broken

I realize that some of you might say, I know that there is something for me to finish. I know that God desires to instruct me in my assignment but I am stuck in circumstance. Listen, I've been there. I've been in that place that I knew God had called me for His purpose but it was knowing how to get up from failure that I needed instructions. God will instruct you in ALL things. About 9 years ago, I was facing the greatest trial of my life. I was just about to give up. I wanted to breakout, but I felt helpless. One day God spoke to me and said, "You are coming out of this but you must follow my instructions." The place I was in was indeed a valley experience, the enemy was coming not only for my mind, but for my life.

My back was against the wall, and my life seemed to be

shattered. That day God spoke to me, He gave me divine

instructions for restoration. He was very clear and detailed.

He told me if I followed His instructions, He would put the

pieces back together. I was desperate. I listened and I

obeyed. His instructions, though simple, challenged me. I

was challenged to crucify the part of me that wanted to

self-medicate and speed up God's process. I needed to kill

the part of me that wanted to do what God said my way.

Daily I had to crucify my flesh, my rebellion, my pride,

and follow His instructions. His instructions were an

already proven victory long before I had the problem. I had

to train my mind, and discipline myself by faith, to not

deviate from God's way to restoration and healing for my

life. I'm a witness that His instructions are essential and

they work. Now, I'm healed, I'm free, I'm restored, and

I'm running to finish, all because I listened and obeyed God's victorious instructions. I have no doubt in my mind that I would not have made it out, had I not followed God's instructions. For everything that the enemy tries to form in your life, if it can form, it can be broken. God's instructions will break the distractions that the enemy seeks to use as hindrances to what God has purposed for your life. Don't allow what God has the power to break to be your hold up. I pray now in Jesus name, that you will seek God for His plan that will pull you out of every valley that you are in. I pray that you will pray and seek God without ceasing. You will not be bound by your circumstance. I pray that your ears are opened to hear clearly, and that the chaos around you will not hinder you from hearing and receiving the solution to every dilemma in your life, in Jesus Name! You are too important to quit, slow down, procrastinate, or to be stuck. You have a right and the power to press forward. Push past the crowd. Get God's word for your life and situation. Be determined, in all things, for all things, and all situations. God has the instructions for you! Get the instructions!

Let us Pray

Heavenly father,

I thank you for your love that guides us. I thank you for your divine instruction that is a lamp to our feet and a light to our path. Father, I pray now that we will be wise enough to comply with Proverbs 3:5-6 which tells us to *"Trust in the Lord with all your heart and lean not to your own understanding, but in all your ways acknowledge Him and He will direct your path."*

May we also take delight in Proverbs 16:9 that says, *"The mind of a man plans his way, but the Lord establishes his steps.* Father we need your instructions for our life. I pray for any person that has been moving without your order. For we know God, that in order to recover, we must have instructions to pursue. Father, when we receive your instructions, I pray for obedience. I pray that we will be willing as well as obedient. According to Isaiah 1:9, we will eat the good of the land. I thank you God that we will receive, heed to, and carry out your instructions for our lives. We will trust in you, and will be anxious for nothing, we will learn to wait for you. We remain in you, by moving with you. We submit our will, ways, and plans to you. We make an exchange with you. Lord, let your will be done in us, and through us.

In Jesus' name,

Amen

Journal your thoughts

_____

_____

_____

_____

_____

_____

_____

_____

_____

_____

_____

_____

_____

"The plan of God is the only perfect route we will ever take. The details won't always be good, but the outcome will be."

-Pastor Deona Benson

Chapter Two

Get The Plan

Habakkuk 2:2 (NLT) Then the Lord said to me, write my answer plainly on tablets, so that a runner can carry the correct message to others.

You heard what the Lord said, now what are you going to do with what he said? To every instruction, it is important to get a plan of action. The instruction might be viewed as the what, whereas the plan of action is more detailed according to the where and the when.

Last year God instructed me to start a mentorship program/ministry. This was an area that I'd unconsciously been working in for quite some time. While meditating one day, God began to speak to me about this ministry. He gave me the name and the assignment at the same time. After receiving the instruction for the mentorship ministry, I had to further seek God to receive the plan of action. I heard what He wanted me to do, now I needed to know how to go about doing what He was calling me to. I had never done this before, and I needed a plan of action to mobilize the instruction.

Jeremiah 29:11 (NLT)

For I know the plans that I have for you declares the Lord. They are plans for good and not for disaster to give you a future and a hope.

Don't be overwhelmed by the instructions. God will give you a precise plan of action. God not only wants to give you what to do, He also wants to give you how to do it! Remember, there is no error in God, and His leading will keep error from you.

God is so brilliant and so creative, and His spirit is on the inside of you, giving you vision and insight that will cause you to flourish beyond your own ability. God desires to show His brilliance through you. He desires to shine so bright through you that everything you do causes the earth to give Him praise. He's a BIG God and He wants to do BIG things through you. Don't be intimidated when His plan of action breaks boundaries and limitations. His plan might sit you before kings and queens. His plan might cause you to apply for positions you don't qualify for. He is not bound by this world or its system, and because you possess Him, neither are you.

The mistake we often make is comparing God's plan to our ability. God's plan will never match your ability. His plan sits at a level that can only be reached with faith.

Ask yourself, "How much faith do I need for what I am doing?" God's plans for your life keeps you reaching for his ability. You will never be sufficient for what God has called you to do.

We are graced to finish what we are graced to start

It is not the will of God that you finish everything that you are currently doing. Every good idea is not a God idea, and just because you're doing it doesn't mean it is purposed for your life. First, if you are currently pursuing something, are you pursuing based on instructions, or are you experimenting? We are only experimenting when we live life without instructions. Everything that has been proven to work is not purposed for you to work it. The grace is on what is ordained for your life. Don't get me wrong, there are millions of people that have experienced success without ever uttering a word of prayer. There are atheist that are millionaires, however we don't want to create success that has no eternal blessing attached to it. The atheist might live as a millionaire, but the finishers' affections are on the crown that is laid up after this life. Our pursuit through all that we do is the kingdom of God and his righteousness. Our affections are on things eternal, our passionate pursuit is heaven's agenda. Real success is when we lay hold of God's heart and His plan for our lives. Only what we do for Christ will last.

Proverbs 16:3 (NLT)

Commit your actions to the Lord and your plans will succeed.

Job 5:8 (ESV)

I will seek God, and to God would I commit my cause.

There must be an inward passion to pursue Christ on the inside of us. Our lives must be yielded to God completely and totally. We must make the exchange of our plans for God's plans.

Even if what you are doing seems to be working, are you humble enough to ask God if what you are doing is in line with His plan for your life? God's plan provides a resting place for His people. We are not testing something out when we follow God's plan, rather we are walking out what has already been tested and proven. Goodness and mercy is attached to His plan. With His plan, we can have confidence in the results.

Psalms 23:6 (KJV)

Surely goodness and mercy shall follow me all the days of my life.

Listen to God's voice for your journey

Proverbs 15:22 (ESV)

Without counsel plans fail, but with many advisers they succeed.

It is important to have people that can pour into you, people of faith that will pray for you, and with wisdom, will advise you. However, our ultimate pursuit should be the direction of the Holy Spirit as we listen for His voice through man.

Proverbs 19:20-21(ESV)

Listen to advice and accept instruction that you may gain wisdom in the future. Many are the plans in the mind of a man, but it is the purpose of the Lord that will stand.

God's plan is for stability and security. His plan is for provision and success. Trust me, God does not want us to fail. Remember, what He purposed us to do is for His name sake. When you fail, He knows that it is His name that takes the hit. Don't allow the process to frustrate you and cause you to become anxious. This journey is bringing you to an expected end. Victory is the expectation.

Prayer gives birth to the plan

Those that trust the Lord rely on His grace and wisdom. We know that it is He who prepares us for every good work. We are not sufficient of ourselves. We depend on Him to establish all of our plans.

The instructions of God and every plan of action must come through prayer. Prayer is essential in our journey. Nothing succeeds without it. It's our opportunity to not only share our hearts with God, but it's also the privilege we have to hear His. Prayer is not a monologue, it is a dialogue. Don't become so anxious in prayer to tell God what you feel, that you don't stick around to get His response. God will respond. Let nothing distract your access to God through prayer. A.B. Simpson wrote, "Prayer is the link that connects us to God." We must stay connected to God. We cannot follow what we cannot hear. Pursue His plans with passion through prayer and watch His plans prevail.

What a sweet privilege it is that God would communicate with us, and reveal to us His secrets, and trust our hands with His plans.

Daniel 2:22 (NIV)

He reveals deep and hidden things. He knows what lies in darkness and light dwells with Him.

Who wouldn't want to talk to the God who knows all. He's El Elyon, the Most High God.

Isaiah 46:10 (NIV)

"I make known the end from the beginning."

The NLT of that verse says, *"Only I can tell you the future before it even happens. Everything will come to pass for I do whatever I wish.*

Hallelujah! We serve the all wise God. The sovereign God that can do whatever He wants. Take rest in the God that leads you. Take rest and cast away all rebellion. He knows what lies ahead, what distractions are going to come, and what schemes and tactics the enemy is going to try to use to get you off course. In His plan, there is an escape route for every plot of the enemy. His plan comes with His power, and that power is not only able to keep you from falling, but will also keep you in safety.

His authority is on His plans, and with that authority, every enemy that comes against the fulfillment and fruit of your assignment will be brought down.

His plan is to prosper you

2 Kings 4 talks about the widow woman whose husband died leaving bad debt. She told the Prophet Elisha that the creditors were coming to take her sons in order to satisfy the debt. Elisha asked her a simple question, and that question was, "What do you have in your house?" She told Elisha that all she had was a jar of oil. Elisha gave her the instruction to go borrow vessels from everywhere she could think of. "Get plenty," he instructed. He said, then come back home, close the door behind you and your sons, and start filling the jars with oil. She did all that Elisha instructed her to do. The scripture reports that as she was filling the jars she called out to one of her sons for him to

give her another jar. Her son said, there are no more. She reported back to Elisha that she filled all the jars with oil. He then gave her a further plan of action. He told her to go sell her oil, and pay her debt. Then he said, after you pay your debt, live off of what remains. She was given a plan of action that saved her life.

There is somebody reading this, and the plan that God wants to give you is more than simple instructions, it's a plan to save your life and restore your situation. He wants to give you a plan to cancel debt. He wants to give you a plan that will pull you out of the dry place you are in. He wants to give you a plan that will accelerate you, one that will catapult you into places you never imagined you would go.

There was a season that I was frustrated and unfulfilled. I felt stuck. I felt that there was greater calling me, but the giants of circumstance seemed to have had me barricaded. I had gone to God like the widow woman seeking help. I needed answers. I was searching for access into the greater that I believed to be purpose for my life. I was mentally and financially broken, seemingly doors were shut around me. One day in prayer God ministered to me telling me that He was trying to get my eyes off of the external doors. He told me, now is the time for you to tap into the internal doors that possess the overflow that you are searching for, and not the opportunities that are created for you. He said, I'm teaching you how to create opportunity. He took me to this very scripture and showed me how I'd been crying and complaining about what was against me. He asked me the question that would change my life, "What is in your house?"

He then assured me that He was not withholding the open doors from me. He said, "I have called you to be a door."

It's time that you work what's on the inside of you so that it can work for you. Many of you are stuck because you are waiting to walk through doors, while God is trying to open a door in you.

What do you have in your house? What plan is God trying to give you for what you have in your hand? Though seemingly insignificant, could it be that what you have is the oil of prosperity?

Deuteronomy 8:18 tells us to remember the Lord, for it is He who gives us the power to get wealth. God is not trying to withhold wealth and riches from His people. The enemy has given us a false humility, causing us to believe that success is linked to pride, and lowliness and humility means living on barely. Not so, Psalms 35:27 has us to know that the Lord takes pleasure in our prosperity. We are in His image and in His likeness. It is His will that we live abundantly. Only the thief comes to kill, steal, and destroy, but Christ said, I come that you not only have life, but an abundant life. God wants to expand what's in your hand. He's trying to add to you. As your fruit is multiplied, His name is glorified.

His plans and abilities are so great, and you are a product of His brilliance. Who can transform death to life, but God? Who can cause what has already been born to be born again but God? His plan translated you into a heavenly kingdom even though you exist here on earth. His plan has seated you together with Christ in heavenly places (Ephesians 2:4-7). His plan has given you power over all the power of the enemy (Luke 10:19). If you ever wrestle with the plan of God, consider the life in Christ it has afforded you already. His way is life. You are a living witness.

Plan to be patient

The friend to God's plan is patience. Don't be in a hurry. God's plan is for purpose, and purpose must stay one with time. The enemy comes to distract purpose by frustrating us with time. When we are distracted, so is our ability to hear God. Satan wants to get you off course. He wants to keep us out of the will of God, he knows that the blessing of the Lord comes by being in the will of the Lord. Distractions, frustration, and impatience come as opposing forces to keep us from the will of God, ultimately because he doesn't want you to gain the blessing. He wants to hinder your fruit. Stay focused. Discipline your mind with the word of God. Wait on him with patience. Let nothing, or no one distract you from the plan of God. From salvation to the very details of our walk with Him, there is

a divine plan. Work it! It will work for you!

Let us Pray

Heavenly Father,

Your word says in Jeremiah 29:11, you know the plans you have for us, and those plans are for good, and not for disaster. They are to give us a future and hope. Father, we take delight in your plans, seek your plans, and we pursue your plans. Father, you have given us the ability to be creative and innovative. You created us with brilliance and intellect. Many gifts, talents, and abilities you have given us to edify your body and the earth. Yet we commit all of our plans to you, according to Proverbs 16:3. We look to you for approval and establishment. You have created us from greatness for greatness, and greatness, we shall witness. Father, we give every idea, every agenda, every thought, and every plan back to you. We ask that you lead, guide, and direct us. It is our desire that our steps are ordered and that our way is successful. It is in you that we live, in you that we move, and in you that we have our being. We thank you for perfecting our plans and for giving us the grace to both execute and accomplish all that you have set before us.

In Jesus' Name,

Amen

Journal your thoughts

_____

_____

_____

_____

_____

_____

_____

_____

_____

_____

_____

_____

_____

_____

_____

_____

_____

_____

_____

_____

_____

_____

_____

_____

_____

_____

_____

_____

_____

"Give me six hours to chop down a tree and I will spend the first four sharpening the axe."

-Abraham Lincoln

Chapter Three

Get Prepared

PROVERBS 24:27

Prepare your work outside; get everything ready for

yourself in the field, and after that build your house.

One of the most important things a runner will do is to

prepare for the race.

Preparation by definition is to make something ready for

use or consideration. Are you ready for use? Often times

we anticipate what we are not ready for. The instruction is

clear, the plan is in place, but are you in position?

Preparation proves our faith in God's instruction.

Preparation is an act of submission and obedience.

Preparation says, "I expect success." If you want to show God faith, show Him preparation. Ephesians 3:20 says, God is able to do exceedingly, abundantly, above all what we ask or think. As we walk out what God has said, we must prepare for exceeding results. Prepare for God to manifest bigger than you can imagine, and He will!

Don't allow fear to enter the equation. Fear hinders preparation. Fear comes not only to delay, but fear comes to cause you to abort assignments. Fear is present to destroy your potential. It causes what's ahead of you to look bigger than the power of your faith. It makes those that do not believe in you seem relevant to the details of your success. Fear causes you to take your eyes off of the power of God and place them on your circumstance. Can you trust if God has called you to stand up to Goliath, that He sees in you a David? If only we would give God our unwavering faith without conditions every time He spoke to us, could you imagine what we could accomplish?

Could you imagine the impact we would have in the earth

if we just gave God a "Yes" and began to prepare from the

moment He gave us His instruction?

Are you prepared to carry out the will of God His way,

trusting and relying on Him without distractions? Are you

prepared to run with what you have been given? Weariness

comes more quickly to those who are unprepared. Prepare

for the test and challenges that might come to slow you

down. Prepare your heart for possible interruptions.

Prepare your mind to be fixed on what God said regardless

of what you might face contrary to His word. Prepare to be

steadfast and unmovable that you might continue to

abound in every good work.

You want to be an author. Are you prepared to write? You

want to go back to school, are you prepared to be a

student? You want to preach, but are you prepared through

personal study and prayer to deliver a fresh word to God's people. It's possible that though we are ready, we are not always prepared for what we feel we are ready for.

Take time to prepare. Prepared people are progressive people and progressive people become prosperous people. We are living in a time where we want the promise, but reject the process. Don't wait until you see it. Prepare for it right now!

Opportunity to the unprepared is a bag with holes in it. Preparation is key to foundation.

Prepare to pursue. Let's looks at the definition again.

Prepare: *to make something ready for use or consideration.* Catch it! It takes faith to prepare. Preparation is faith. Not only does preparation get ready for the known, preparation says just in case there is more to be had, I'm going to be prepared for that too. Are you faithful enough to prepare for consideration? Are you faithful enough to prepare not just for promises, but for possibilities.

Preparation proves expectation. If you expect your plans to succeed, then prepare. Don't just be ready. Be prepared. Dress for success. Your speech, your actions, your posture, should all prove preparation. If God has given vision, then you must prepare for what He has shown you.

Beware of the battlefield of the mind

It starts in the mind. Visions and dreams must be accomplished first in the mind, so they can take seat in the heart. It is important to guard your mind and heart by what you take in through your eyes and ears. Without accomplishing vision for victory in your mind, what comes up against you in the race will shake you. Opposition will slow you down, even sit you down. Accomplish victory in your mind, establish victory in your heart, and be steadfast.

Prepare to see what God has shown you. Mark 11:24

instructs us to believe that we have received in the moment

of prayer. It is yours if God has shown you anything. If

you are believing God for anything, according to His word,

it's yours! Don't waiver!

James 1:6-8 (NLT)

But when you ask him, be sure that your faith is in God

alone. Don't waiver, for a person with divided loyalty is as

unsettled as a wave of the sea that is blown and tossed by

the wind. Such people should not expect to receive

anything from the Lord. Their loyalty is divided between

God and the world and they are unstable in everything

they do.

You've got to grasp it in your mind. Choose to believe!

Without condition, ignore all circumstance. Don't waiver

in your faith. Stability receives the blessing. Stay focused on the finish and prepare for the prize. There is a reward of victory now, and we know there is a crown of life after this!

Burn out, weariness, frustration, and even quitting comes when our focus is lost, and when our faith waivers, and when we place on ourselves what God himself will provide. Our fight is from victory. Prepare for victory. What are you saying? What are you listening to? What are you doing? Your environment and your attachments are key. Don't let the noise around you get in you. Protect the ground of your mind. Be careful of what seeds are sown. Wrong seeds planted in your mind will hinder good fruit from growing in your life.

Be intentional

Get up! You can't sleep through the race. God revealed it to you. Your potential is trying to break out! It requires your participation. It requires your preparation.

Luke 14:28 (ESV)

For which of you, desiring to build a tower does not first sit down and count the cost whether he has enough to complete it.

Preparation is availability. Preparation causes us to be accessible, flexible, and accountable to God. Have you counted up the cost? Preparation counts up the cost.

One of the greatest dangers of pursuing is moving unprepared. Get ready for where you are going. Get your plan in hand, get the blueprint together.

Who knows when the flood gates of abundance will open on your behalf? Any day now, it could happen! Are you prepared for it?

Maybe you are about to open a daycare. Perhaps there are no children now, but you have gotten the instruction and you have gotten the plan of action. Are your prepared for the daycare to be filled suddenly? Are you prepared for your business to take off?

Preparation is not motivated by sight. Preparation is fueled by faith. To be prepared is to be empowered and equipped for God's use. Don't allow the lack of preparation to hinder your potential.

You are ready, but are you prepared? Great things happen when opportunity meets preparation.

Proverbs 6:6-8 (ESV)

Go to the ant, O sluggard; consider her ways, and be wise. Without having any chief, officer, or ruler, she prepares her bread in summer and gathers her food in harvest.

Let us Pray

Heavenly Father,

We thank you for the wisdom to prepare for the race. We take the time to count up the cost in all things that you have required of us. We actively participate by faith and preparation. We prepare our hearts and minds for victory. We prepare for the possible battles. We prepare for the storms that might come by accomplishing victory by faith. We set our hopes on you. We look to you, the author and the finisher of our faith.

We remain focused on your Word. We mix our faith with your word, and our action with our faith. We shall see the goodness of the Lord in the land of the living. We prepare for the goodness that shall be seen.

May our preparation prove our expectation, and may our expectation bring manifestation.

In Jesus Name,

Amen

Journal your thoughts

_____

_____

_____

_____

_____

_____

_____

_____

_____

_____

_____

_____

_____

_____

Chapter Four

Get Started

Ephesians 2:10 (NLT)

For we are God's masterpiece. He has created us anew in

Christ Jesus, so we can do the good things he planned for

us to do long ago.

You were created for such a time as this. You were

purposefully placed here on earth for the task that is set

before you. What is set before you has been prepared for

you, it's awaiting your arrival. The prepared work, now

needs a mobile prepared you.

For every dream, vision, and assignment, there must be

consistent mobility that will breathe life into its possibility.

Think big, stretch out, and move out. Desire is good. Faith

is a must, but along with faith, you have to move. Dreams can be big and beautiful, but if you are going to see it, you have to wake up from that dream and walk it out.

When God shares his heart with ours, He is revealing to us heaven's desire and its readiness to release in the earth. What a privilege and honor that heaven has prepared its work for you. How humbling it is to know that you were chosen for the good works of Christ. Heaven needed a vehicle to transport purpose, and you were chosen to be that vehicle.

Though broken, sinful, and unworthy heaven chose you. We who were alienated from Christ, with hearts full of evil and wickedness, God chose to reveal in us His son. (Galatians 1:15). He chose to give our shattered lives hope and purpose. His purpose is divine. He's intentional and what is on the inside of you is for purpose, on purpose, and with purpose. You are a significant part of the puzzle. It's wrong thinking to feel as if anybody can do what you were created to do. Ephesians 2:10 says, you were created for the work. Take a minute and think on that. God has a purpose, a good work prepared. He looked at the work and saw who the work needed. He considered what type of personality, skill, gifting, talents, and temperament would be needed for the work, and He formed you. Yes! He formed you! There is no question if you are the one. You were the one created specifically for what God has set before you. He did not set the work before you and say, "Here it is." He sat you before the work and said, here he/she is. Here they are, the one who will bring you to completion. Here they are, the one whose hands are equipped to hold you. Here they are, the one whose shoulders are built to carry you, and the one whose legs will walk you out. Here is the breath that will cause you to have life.

God has spoken, now mobilize on what He has said.

Procrastination, the silent killer

Procrastination and fear both kill mobility. Do not give

them room! When there is no mobility, there is no harvest.

Proverbs 20:4(ESV)

The sluggard does not plow in the autumn, he will seek at

harvest and have nothing.

Most procrastinators are frustrated by the lack of fruit in

their lives. They are unfulfilled and settling beneath their

ability, and the truth is, their own slothfulness is one of the

greatest giants to their success.

Proverbs 20:13 (ESV)

Love not sleep lest you come to poverty. Open your eyes

and you will have plenty of bread.

Procrastination is purpose assassination. Don't allow slothfulness to assassinate the progress of your purpose. Procrastination doesn't always travel alone, it is often accompanied by fear. It is fear of the unknown, fear of not being good enough, fear of failure, or fear of success. Fear can also be referred to as the liar. There is no truth in fear. Fear is deception and it is from the enemy.

2 Timothy 1:7 (KJV)

God did not give us the spirit of fear, but of power, and of love, and a sound mind.

Fear is everything that is not real. It is everything that has no power. If the enemy can grip you with fear, he knows that even if you are mobile, you will not be steadfast and effective. Fear keeps us fruitless. One writer said, "Fear kills more dreams than failure ever will." If your life is going to bear fruit, you must move in faith knowing that God is with you and there is no failure in Him. My Bishop, a very wise man of God, Bishop Roderick Mitchell once said, "We don't want to do anything for God, because trying to do things for Him brings failure. We want to do it with God. When we do God's work with Him, we bear much fruit and bring success.

You've already won the race

When God releases His instruction, it is tied to an already victory. It is not for a possible victory, it is for an already victory. What is before you, is already! It is already victorious. You are already successful. There is no need to fear and no need to be frustrated. Rest in knowing that it is Already! Don't allow procrastination and fear to get together and keep you stuck! If you are reading this, and you are being gripped by the enemy of procrastination and the lies of fear, I pray right now in the name of Jesus that the grips of Satan are broken off your life. I bind up every tormenting spirit, every lazy spirit, every complacent spirit, and all excuses; by the power of the Holy Ghost we detach and disconnect every thought and imagination that seeks to come against the truth and knowledge of Christ from your mind and thoughts now.

You will no longer give in to excuses that are provoked by procrastination and fear. I declare that your eyes are opened! You are awakened. Everything, everyone, every power, and every principality that stands against your mobility in the purpose of Christ, is brought down to nothing now in Jesus' name. Every scheme, every plot, every ploy, every bit of reasoning, every thought from the enemy, we call it ineffective, and we take it captive and bring it into the obedience of Christ. Your mind is free.

Your feet are no longer bound by slothfulness. You are no

longer held hostage by fear, but you are now free. Every

hidden weight is exposed and removed now, and you are

abounding in the work of the Lord bearing much fruit, and

fruit that remains in Jesus mighty name, Amen.

Hallelujah! You are ready now! Know this, purpose is not

running from you. She is not hiding herself or trying to

play hard to get. She is accessed by mobility. If you are to

ever finish the work, you must mobilize the plans. What is

waiting on your mobility? It is time to get started. Destiny

is calling you. You have received God's instructions, his

plans of action, and you are prepared.

Now get started! Whatever the work God set you before,

get started! Don't be hindered or delayed by anything.

Don't allow another day, week, month, or year to pass you

by. Empty yourself out. Be healed and set free from

addictions. Be healed and set free of past pain, abuse, rejection, and disappointment. Be healed and set free of the guilt and shame of your error and mistakes. Turn to God, lean, trust, and depend on him, and get busy living! Get busy running! You are still breathing and so should your dreams, visions, and God's purpose for your life. Persevere, don't bow to challenges. Fight the good fight of faith and live abundantly. It is through Christ that you will accomplish everything (Philippians 4:13). It is not over; there is more for you to do. You are the bread for someone's life, who's starving because you are not moving. You are the light for someone's life who's in darkness because you are sitting still. You have a to-do list and you have got to fulfill it. Something needs your push to be delivered into the earth. Tell unfruitfulness goodbye! Tell lack goodbye! So long fears! So long excuses! So long emptiness! Get up from there; there is greatness inside of you, greatness that cannot be summed up by what is on your family tree. It is bigger than that. What is in you comes off of the tree of your heavenly father. The earth awaits your coming and all nature anticipates your reveal. Your voice must be heard, your wisdom and insight must be read, your testimony is needed, your hands must be felt, and your feet must impact territory. Let's go! We have been given only a little while. It is time to mobilize! Let's make the most of every opportunity! I believe by faith that there is a stirring in the spirit realm concerning you even as you read this book. I pray for open doors and new opportunities to extend to you now. From this day forward you will see yourself as God sees you, and you will run in his strength. I speak that your faith is renewed. Your vision is clear and your eyes are open! You are breaking through and breaking out!

Pour yourself out faithfully! Out of your belly will flow rivers of living water. Everything your hands touch will prosper.

John 9:4 (AMP)

We must work the works of him who sent me and be busy with his business while it is daylight; night is coming when no man can work.

Do not spend another day saying what you would, could, or should do. The time is now to buy up every opportunity and fulfill God's purpose for your life. You are obligated to God's purpose! Get an "I Must" down in your spirit. Your life is no longer your own. You were bought with a price. Lace up your shoes. It's time to mobilize the vision. What are you going to do with the breath you have left?

Ecclesiastes 11:4 (AMP)

He who watches the wind [waiting for all conditions to be perfect] will not sow [seed], and he who looks at the clouds will not reap [a harvest]

Let us Pray

Heavenly Father,

We thank you now for the courage to move out with you, knowing that we have no need to fear. You are a very present help in trouble. You are with us even in the valley and your word says you are with us always! God, I thank you that we are not bound by procrastination and fear. Fear has lost its grip. Every lie has been exposed and every hindering thing has been revealed and removed. There are no excuses. We are healed and set free. We are ready and open. We are willing and obedient. We are faithful and fruitful. We are stable in our mobility. Our work will bring glory to your name. We are abounding in you in all things. We declare that we will not be robbed another day of our life.

In Jesus' name,

Amen.

Journal your thoughts

_____

_____

_____

_____

_____

_____

_____

_____

_____

_____

_____

_____

_____

_____

_____

_____

_____

_____

_____

_____

_____

_____

_____

_____

_____

_____

_____

_____

_____

_____

"The race has its challenges, but whatever you do, don't stop running!"

-Pastor Deona Benson

Chapter Five

Get Finished

2 Corinthians 8:11(ISV)

Now finish what you began, so that your eagerness to do

so may be matched by your eagerness to complete it.

We have arrived at the very inspiration of this book. My

life has changed by this simple yet profound revelation. I

now have a greater passion, to not only pursue purpose,

but to run until I finish. I am sober minded and alert. My

armor is on and secure.

It is my prayer, that by this chapter you too are refreshed in

your focus, and inspired to not only pursue, but to run and

finish your course. Many great people with great ideas and

dreams have fallen, not because of what they carried, but simply because they did not seek God on how to carry what they had been given. God figured it all out for us. It has all been prepared. He will guide us if we would only allow Him.

I was inspired and given the instructions to write this book after preaching a message titled "Get Finished." The message was inspired by 2 Timothy 4:7-9 (KJV)

"I have fought a good fight, I have finished my course. I have kept the faith and hence forth there is laid up for me a crown of righteousness, which the Lord, the righteous judge shall give me at that day and not to me only but unto all them also that love his appearing."

When I read that scripture, (one that I had read and heard countless times) for the first time, I read it as a message of encouragement to keep running. I'd seen the scripture so much in relation to death, but for the first time, it was a message that spoke life. Paul was nearing his end, and as

he gave instruction and exhortation to Timothy, he

encourages Timothy by saying you have got to keep

running. My run is coming to an end. I stayed the course

and completed the work that was set before me. My first

thought was, what a beautiful privilege to be able to look

back over your life and say, "I got finished!" Far too many

people have died and yet full with potential on the inside

of them. Far too many legacies are in the grave. As I stood

before that congregation admonishing them to be steadfast

in the work of the Lord, building up those who had fallen

out of the race by way of circumstance, reviving weary

hearts with the word of God; something began to stir up on

the inside of me like never before. A realization and a

greater revelation of Christ and his purpose for my own

life began to expand and release in my heart in a way that

would cause me not only to write this book, but others that I am purposed to write.

 My passion to preach the gospel increased.

Isaiah 61:1-3 (ISV) laid as a pavement under my feet:

The Spirit of the Lord is upon me, because the LORD has anointed me; he has sent me to bring good news to the oppressed and to bind up the brokenhearted, to proclaim freedom for the captives, and release from darkness for the prisoners to proclaim the year of the LORD's favor, the day of vengeance of our God; to comfort all who mourn; to provide for those who grieve in Zion- to bestow on them a crown of beauty instead of ashes, the oil of gladness instead of mourning, a mantle of praise instead of a spirit of despair." "Then the people will call them "Oaks of Righteousness", "The planting of the Lord", in order to display his splendor.

My feet hit this pavement and I began to run with a clearer focus. I realized that where I was is where I belonged. It was my right because it was God's purpose for my life. I stood more confident in my position. I realized in that moment, I was born for this. I am a product of the Lord's doing! He called me for such a time as this and without apologies, compromise, or excuses, I gave God a new yes and vowed with diligence, obedience and passion, that I will GET FINISHED!

I vowed never again to allow any amount of opposition distract my faith nor my fight.

Not only did I purpose in my heart to finish my course as it relates to divine assignments but to every purpose that I have been called. As a person, a wife, a mother, I made up in my mind that with purpose in every step I would fulfill and bring to completion everything that I'd begun according to the will of God for my life. With integrity and excellence, I purposed to close all gaps present in my life.

We as believers are required to be good stewards over

what God has given and entrusted unto us. God is counting

on us to represent Him well.

This message would cause me to pursue with a greater

passion, pray longer, push harder, persevere, and be

steadfast. I left that day considering how many people are

wasting away, existing and not truly living. How many are

down on their face due to persecution and affliction that

the word warned us would come?

I left with a burden of just how many people have never

embraced or even given thought to the possibilities and

potential that is on the inside of them. Too many people

are living day to day being tossed about by situation and

circumstance, being driven by the forces of life. Too many

are up one minute and down the next, with wondering

minds, wavering faith, and wasting potential. Suddenly I

felt a call to sound an alarm that would stir up the gifts, passions, potential, and purpose inside of God's people just as the stirring had begun in me. You belong here. You are significant and you've got to run with the intent to finish. The beginning is not good enough, doing something is not good enough, putting your time in here a little and there a little is not good enough. Heaven has an agenda for our lives. We can no longer allow hindrances to allow the day to dissipate, resulting in missed moments and opportunities for the gospel to get out, the kingdom to be advanced, and God to be glorified through us on earth. Regardless of where you are right now, there is more for you to do! God has equipped you to endure to the finish line. God wants to fire, fuel, and stir you up in such a way that you are in motion with excitement!

Obstacles, opposition, closed doors, trials, fiery darts, temptations, attacks, affliction, feeling alone, and feeling bombarded, are all a part of the journey. They will develop you or they will distract you. You choose what place they will hold. Don't let them break you. Allow them to build you. You will laugh, you will cry, you will hurt, you will feel pressure, you will see what looks like defeat, but through it all, you will experience victory, but you have to keep going! Circumstance will try to choke the life out of you, but you shall live and you shall not die. Weapons are going to form. You will find yourself in the valley, you will face giants, you will come through rising water and fire, but you will not be overtaken! You will not be consumed. Your faith must remain in Christ and while you stand on the word, there must be a determination to get finished. You cannot give out halfway through, you have to keep running. Dust failure off and keep running. When you fall, people will try to hold you in that place. Do not be held by condemnation to what grace pulls you from.

God's grace is indeed sufficient for your life (2

Corinthians 12:9). We are not fighting for victory, we are

fighting from victory. I said earlier in the book, you are a

let there be! Nothing is more powerful than a let there be

out of God's mouth! What he calls, shall be! You can't go

so low that you undo God's let there be! Hell cannot undo

God's let there be. Situations cannot undo God's let there

be, and you have a let there be inside of you.

Ask Paul (Acts 18) rejection will come, but what do you

do when you are rejected? You keep running! God is with

you to protect you and his purpose inside of you. Maybe

you are reading this and you feel that you have ran all you

could. You are not quite sure you can endure another

painful blow to your pursuit. I wrote this book to tell you,

you can make it! You can! You will and you must! You

are not in this alone. I know you feel lonely, but you are

not alone. Even in the fire, God is with you. David said in

Psalms 23, *"I will fear no evil for thou art with me."* God is running with you. He's standing beside you. He will give you a second wind. God is saying *come to me, all who labor and are heavy laden and I will give you rest. Take my yoke upon you and learn from me. For I am gentle and lowly in heart, and you will find rest for your souls. For my yoke is easy and my burden is light (Matthew 11:28-30 ESV).* God's prepared work is not meant to kill you or beat you down. He says my way is easy. He gives us peace beyond our comprehension. He's God, He will not be out done. God who called you to it, will not only see you through conception, but He is with you in delivery. There is pain in the push, but push anyway.

Philippians 1:6 (KJV)

"He that has begun a good work in you shall perform it until the days of Jesus Christ.

1 Thessalonians 5:24 (KJV)

"Faithful is he who has called you and he will also bring

it to pass.

You are more than what comes easy for you. God put an ability to fight on the inside of you. The bible says you are more than a conqueror through him that loves you (Romans 8:37). Your family needs you.

Your community, your church, your city, the nation, and all the earth awaits your impact, the forceful impact of your steps on the pavement and your unstoppable mobility!

1 Corinthians 9:24 (NLT)

"Don't you realize that in a race everyone runs but only

one person gets the prize, So run to win! All athletes are

disciplined in their training. They do it to win a prize that

will fade away, but we do it for an eternal prize. So, I run with purpose in every step. I am not just shadow boxing. I discipline my body like an athlete training it to do what it should, otherwise, I fear that after preaching to others I myself might be disqualified."

Here, Paul said, there is discipline in finishing. He said I have purpose in every step! Wow! How powerful! How much purpose is in your steps? How intentional are you about every move you make? You are much too significant, much too valuable not to realize that your steps have influence whether they are purposed or not. What influence are your steps making? Someone is watching. Someone is following. Where do your steps lead those that are coming behind you? In 2 Timothy 2, Paul was able to show and tell Timothy to look at his footsteps, follow them, and to get finished with your portion of the race.

Where are your steps going? By what inspiration, leading, and guiding, do you walk? Align your feet with the path God has set before you! You cannot stop until you reach finish. We don't get to mark our finish, only destiny can do that.

I speak life into you. I speak joy into you. If you have lost your passion, I speak fire back into you! I pray that you will pursue more patiently the crown laid up for the finisher. May your strength be renewed.

Like a crowd on the sidelines of a race, so is all of heaven cheering you on! He gives strength to the weary and increases the power of the weak (Isaiah 40:29). Heaven is for you! Abba and the angels are cheering and chanting all at once, "You can do it!" It is because you are in Christ, and through him you can do all things. Only you can do what you were created to do. If you don't do it, then you leave a void.

Hebrews 12:1-2 NLT

"Therefore since we are surrounded by such a huge cloud of witnesses to the life of faith, let us strip off every weight that slows us down especially the sin that so easily trips us up. And let us run with endurance the race God has set before us. We do this by keeping our eyes on Jesus the champion who initiates and perfects our faith. Because of the joy awaiting him, he endured the cross disregarding its shame. Now He is seated in the place of honor beside God's throne!"

In order to finish, I pray that your focus is fixed on the finisher. I am reminded of my own testimony, one by sin and shame, my life seemingly took a turn to defeat. My life was chaotic, I was confused, depressed, suicidal, and stuck. Circumstance had me bound. I was running well, then distraction came. I started off being divided. I was

divided between situation and purpose. Situation

eventually got the best of me, and for a season, situation

determined my steps. I became a slave to what was

supposed to be a slave to me. I sat in a mental state that

allowed opposition to have its foot on my head, although

my foot was called to be on the head of opposition. I

believed the lies that the enemy said about me. I was

condemned by the guilt that Satan would not let me

escape. I was bound because I did not realize that I was

created to finish. I hadn't conceived the truth that Jesus

Christ was my righteousness, and I was hidden in him. My

eyes were on my works, and my works called me a failure.

Thanks be to God who shined the light on that lie, and

revealed His truth about me to me. I had to pull myself up

by faith, take God at His word, and be courageous enough

to fight past, not only my enemy, but also my inner me. It

was out of that dark place that a voice whispered to me, "If you get up and walk, I will get you through this." I found my strength in Him and I got up. Some days were easier than others, but love lifted me. The love of God chased away my fears, and delivered me from oppression and depression. The love of God shined the light on every dark place. His love forgave my offenses and graced me to forgive those that offended me. The enemy wanted me to give up and get out of the race. He taunted me. I felt his anger. I cried out to God, and in the presence of my enemies he led me to the rock that was much higher than I. He was my refuge. He put me in a place where my enemies could not reach me (Psalms *61)*. He put me back in the race and grace caused me to run again. I ran out of every trap of the enemy. God healed me, he delivered me, and he set me free! There is grace for the race! Whatever you need grace to be, it is sufficient. It was the truth that made me free. The truth of who I am THROUGH Christ. The truth revealed that my faith made me whole. We must look and live through Christ. I had to discipline myself to think like a victor and not a victim. Only victors can endure the race, more challenges will come, but victors must keep their eyes on the crown. Victors are led by the spirit and not our flesh! Just because you have fallen does not mean that it's the end of your race. Get back on course and get finished. Make up in your mind that you are going to run with patience and faith. Run with determination! Chin up and heart open, looking to Christ for all of your help.

Galatians 2:20 (KJV)

I am crucified with Christ: nevertheless I live; yet not I, but Christ liveth in me: and the life which I now live in the flesh I live by the faith of the son of God, who loved me, and gave himself for me.

You will finish! Every project, every assignment, every endeavor that is purposed for your life by God, you will get finished. Hell cannot prevail against the finisher. Though hell tries to keep you out and shut you down, it's only fueling your fire and enlarging your boarders. God will not be outdone. You are His possession. He will be made great through your life. Enemies will come, but they will stumble and fall because you are a finisher. You will not be denied because you are a finisher. Empty yourself out! Unleash your greatness in the earth. It was not meant to die with you, it was meant for you to release it, so that long after you are gone, your purpose will be lived through others. Don't hold back! Run with tenacity. Release your oil! Set a fire in the land! The bible says that your gift will make room for you, and as I write I hear God saying He is making room for your gift! The devil thought his plan would work against you, he had no idea it would work for you! We are the Master's piece! A mighty piece of His glorious puzzle. Are you running yet? We are prepared for this! We are forgetting those things which are behind and we are moving towards what is ahead. No fear, all faith! Run out of what was meant to bury you, and build a sanctuary on top of it! Release your let there be, fight the good fight, finish your course, keep the faith and get the crown! On your mark! Get ready! Get set! Go! The earth is waiting!

1 Corinthians 9:24

Do you not know that in a race all runners run, but only

one receives the prize? So, run that you may obtain it!

GET FINISHED!

Let us Pray

Heavenly Father,

We thank you! We are ready to run. By faith with purpose in every step, we are running! Towards the prize, without fear, without hesitation, we are running. We are in motion. We yield our lives to you, and we will fight a good fight. We will stay our course. We will keep the faith and we will run! We will finish! We thank you for increasing our strength. We thank you for healing, deliverance, and breakthrough. We thank you that love is lifting us up, and your power is making us strong. You are instructing us, guiding us, and keeping watch over us. We will live faithfully and fruitfully, abounding in every good work, and buying up every opportunity. There is nothing missing or broken in our lives. We are in the race forward focused, and no longer past possessed. Father, by faith we will endure and be faithful to pour ourselves out empty. We will not be weary in well doing. We know according to your word, that as long as the earth remains there will be seed time and harvest. We place our hope in you. We look to you, as we lift our voices and encourage ourselves in you as we declare, "WE CAN, WE WILL, WE MUST GET FINISHED! Lord, we know that we can do all things through Christ that strengthens us.

In Jesus' Name,

Amen

Write the vision and make it plain

_____

_____

_____

_____

_____

_____

_____

_____

_____

_____

_____

_____

_____

About the Author

Deona Benson, born in Detroit, Michigan. Was raised in Memphis, TN, and she is the daughter of Apostle Darnell and Yma Thompson. She is a 2002 graduate of Kirby High School (Memphis,Tn).

Pastor Deona Benson is the Co-Pastor of the University of Life Church, along with her husband Pastor Dedrick Benson, in Oxford, MS. She is the founder of Beyond the Break Mentorship and Christian Counseling. She is the visionary and host of Me Time Regional Women's Fellowship in the North Mississippi area. It is her passion for souls that keeps her focused, driven, and determined to Get Finished as she travels preaching and teaching the Gospel of Jesus Christ. Together she and her husband have 4 children.

"You will find the beauty of life when you find your purpose for living. When you find it, run until you finish."

-Pastor Deona Benson

Visit www.deonabenson.com for booking and more information.